Warrior

Kylee Bustard

BookLeaf
Publishing

India | USA | UK

Presentation by *BookLeaf Publishing*

Web: www.bookleafpub.com

E-mail: info@bookleafpub.com

ISBN: 978-93-5744-813-0

First edition 2022

DEDICATION

Dedicated to the incredible women in my life.

ACKNOWLEDGEMENT

I would like to express my gratitude to BookLeaf Publishing for giving me this opportunity to release Warrior as my first published poetry book. I give thanks to my closest friend, Grace Lee, for always believing in me and inspiring me to write poetry and find strength in vulnerability. Finally, thank you to my mom, Denise Bustard, for being the compassionate and powerful woman I look up to as a role model.

PREFACE

In her first year of university, Kylee Bustard undertook BookLeaf Publishing's writing challenge #TheWriteAngle. In October of 2021, she wrote 21 poems for 21 days and worked with the company to produce her first published poetry book. Her inspiration was drawn from personal experiences of gender inequality and supporting others with the impacts of sexual assault and mental health struggles. With her story interwoven with the vulnerable hardships of her loved ones, she was given permission by each survivor and warrior to write and release their shared experiences.

Purple Poetry

Prior to
The purple penmanship on paper
The pristine page pleads

Please
Promise me
You'll write powerful poetry
To propel all
Towards equal prosperity
Impartiality
A people purged of patriarchy

The pledge of an empty page
As a platform and a stage
For women
For Pride
For all

Pink Legos

Date night:
Two teens
Staring each other down
Fingers twitching in anticipation
DRAW
They plunge into the pit
The big box of lego blocks

Brows furrowed in concentration
Eyes searching beyond the bulky house frames
Pink and purple blocks
So foreign to his childhood
The odd furniture sets
Lacking prime materials
Confining the imagination
To anything but home design

He sighs

He makes a space station
She builds the aircraft
For her first time
Not a house

The Beast

When I told him of my hero
My loved one
My friend
Of the ghost living on
After her murder
Her will's end

He was quiet
For a moment
Before speaking his mind

How short was that skirt?
How much did she drink?
What did she think
was bound to happen?

The boy became a beast
Of my darkest dreams
As I sat in grief
Refusing to weep

For my pillaged friend
For the eight months I mourned alone
For my mislead trust in the boy
Whom I wanted to call Home

But he was unworthy

Spaghetti Straps

When we were seven
We were told
Don't be so bold
As to let your shorts shrink
Shorter than your fingertips
Held at your sides
Beside your thighs
Was this child sexualization in disguise?

We didn't understand
Why spaghetti straps were a sin
How shoulders were seductive
When 'sex' was still a swear word
Why bra straps at age ten
Were to be hidden
Humiliating

Yet
At age eleven
In alarm
My friend whispered
So discreet
"It's showing"

Shrugging
I mumbled
"They're not going anywhere"

A Girl's First Suit

One day
The time arrived
For a girl's first suit
Something simple
Something cheap
Perhaps something beyond
My normal thrift-store heap

I slipped on
The grey-beige jacket
Tucking in a white-buttoned shirt
Spinning around to find a mirror
Thinking
DAMN
I feel good
It was no bullet-proof suit
But I felt invincible

A Risky Situation

When I mentioned I want
To run in the woods
Rise with the sun
And find footing among the roots
Of the morning dew-covered trees

They blinked
Twice
And in an uncomfortable voice
Declared
That would be unwise

When I asked why
They said with a sigh
Don't put yourself
In risky situations

Well
As a woman
It is a dangerous risk
To simply exist

As if I don't already know
The history of women
In every past generation
Is a survivor not a victim

Called "mistaken"
For believing in
Her right to own her own skin

Why should I live in fear
Unable to cross the street
Unable to look up from my feet
Unable to not feel like a piece of dried meat
Laid before a pack of wolves
Every time I wear a dress in the summer heat

And I do
And I'm ashamed
For feeling this way
When I'm not the one to be blamed

I want to run
I want to flee
I want to be free
In the forest
Far far away from humanity
Where it's just me
And the trees
And the soft
Sweet morning breeze

Tree Rings

8

Her eyes are tree rings
Rich brown like fertile soil
Born of the earth
Each layer evidence
Of every weathered storm
A life's worth of struggle
Carved in her iris
A silent stump
Motionless trunk
In the forest she sees
Through the lens
Of tree rings

 - my sister's strength

Collarbone Conversations

It's uncomfortable when face-to-face discussions
Become collar-bone conversations
She speaks and he listens
Not with his ears but his eyes
As they linger
Below her chin
Her throat
Her neck
Her chest
What ever happened to decent respect?

- when it's scandalous to own breasts

In The Hallway

I'd see a rapist in the hallway
Only every couple of days
In the high school four-ways
My mistaken memorization
Of the safe paths
To get to class
I didn't know what to do
Would you?

When he laughs
With his friends
Oblivious
Undisturbed
Unaware of the pain
He wreaked on this world

My claws and fists
Could bruise and scar that boy
My power and words could shred his name
His reputation
But what would that do?

When the world already knows
Those "accusations"
The denied truth

That a boy
Has raped the world
Starting with
One
Of many girls

Love Melts the Heart

12

It can be difficult to see
Such a strong, hard woman
Melt
Giggle
Become weak in the knees
At the sight of him

Or at least it was for me

My friend
A stranger

Until I realized
It's because she's happy

Selective Hearing

'NO' is not flirty
'NO' is not rude
'NO' is not "try again"
'NO' is not "my good dude, let's get nude"

'NO THANK YOU' is not impolite
'NO THANK YOU' does not mean "sure
alright"
'NO THANK YOU' is not "maybe another
night"
'NO THANK YOU' means "fuck off get lost"

- when men are still toddlers

Constellations

14

To me
The bright red splotches
Slathered across my face
Were not eruptions of pus
Begging to burst
But an array of the night sky
Faint freckles and pink pimples
Became
Constellations

There was no need
To hide
My starlight

Diplomacy

My partner asked
Why I sometimes speak in riddles
Always softening my words
As if they're blows rather than feathers
Carrying an open mind
Like a hitchhiker's pack
When ordering pizza is like talking with a
diplomat

Some people think I'm a gentle
Kind-hearted soul
Or to others I'm a doormat
A rest stop for travelers
To scrape to filth off their soles

When I looked into my love's eyes
My words caught me by surprise
It's my defense
I learned
From the explosive people
Once in my life

Red Flags

I did not know

The red flags
Of a first relationship
The warning signs of toxic traits
The subtleties that serve as a last chance
To leave before the stripping of humanity
The sight of seeing through his layers of lies
That I hope the next generation will have the
power to see
The downwards spiral no girl should drown in at
age fifteen

By mistaking charm for kindness
Stumbling from guilt-tripping
Unpredictable bouts of rage
Objectification of women
Bottled-up frustration
Abandoned trust
Lack of intimacy
Lack of honesty
Lack of safety
Manipulation
Gaslighting
Insecurity
Isolation

Jealousy
Yelling
Fear

Why me?

I did not know

The Possibilities

Get married and have kids
Maybe two or three

My younger cousin said
Sighing dreamily
Perhaps unaware
Of all that she could be

Did you know you can choose
To get married or not
To have kids or not
To have a career
In anything you wish
Like an engineer
Or a scientist
An educator
A politician
A businesswoman
A software designer
A successful author
A passionate artist
A powerful poet

Did you know you can be
A wife and a mother
Whatever you choose

But always recognize
Your possibilities

Oh
She said
With a whole new world
Up ahead

Claustrophobic

Sometimes my skin
Feels like a sack of organs
With bones sticking out
All wrong and deformed
It's uncomfortable
And claustrophobic
Living in my own body

A mirror only shows
As far as a conscience goes

So I close my eyes
And try to recognize
All that it does for me
Then sometimes I'll see
A masterpiece

When You Remember

An unwanted touch
Is like the burning of flesh
From a branding iron

No amount of
Soapy steaming showers
Can wash away the scar

Time will pass
Memory may fade
But the caress of your fingers
As you do up your hair
Or pull on a pair
Of summer shorts
It may remind you

What your body can't forget
When it was no longer yours
When you remember

A Language of Respect

Eventually I learned
To stop apologizing
For what I have no control over
For inconveniences
For the smallest unnecessary things
To not put myself down
When I've done nothing wrong

To stop responding with "no problem"
When I put in the work
For that favour
For that gift
For that deed
To not belittle my effort
My acts of kindness

To try to stop saying "I'm good"
In replace of "NO"
Because I've been taught
I've been trained
I've been told
That "no" is disagreeable and rude
When it is my choice
My consent

Now I must relearn the language

Where I respect myself
And demand such from others

Warrior

When I was five
I wanted to be a warrior
Speeding across the galaxy
For my next mission
My next battle
Another adventure
Saving lives

Years later
I realized
I am a descendent
Of a long line of warriors
For I am the first woman
In at least
Four generations
To not hold the title
Survivor
Branded between my thighs

Their strength
Perseverance
And love
Is why I fight
To honour the greatest warriors
In my life

The Star Maker

The girl kneeled on the edge of the universe
Holding the heavens on her sagging shoulders
Her body waist-deep in darkness

Slowly
Sinking
As the distant stars dimmed
Suns capsized
Too far away to say goodbye

Depression set in
The void pulled her in
Lost in isolation
Yet constantly fighting
Willing stardust and debris
To gather for a million years
Finally forming
A little lamp of light
Rebuilding the galaxy
One star at a time

Why are the greatest miracles
The beautiful people
Who carry the weight of the universe

The Story of Sediment

She stands
From above
Overlooking The Wave
Sheets of sediment
Pushed down by the pressure
After eras of erosion
Smoothed over with the stroke of a paintbrush
Their story of sharp edges
Stratified over centuries
Now hidden beneath the beauty

She stands
On sinking shoulders
Like the layers of the earth
The women
The humble warriors
Who came before her
Worn out by the weight
Set the stable base
For the next set of heroes
The history is not so pretty
But strength comes
From persevering the ugly

She stands
Not alone